BEYOND THE ORDINARY CAMERA

Diane Bair and Pamela Wright

Contents

Rigby
A Harcourt Achieve Imprint

www.Rigby.com
1-800-531-5015

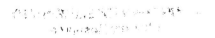

Cameras Are Everywhere

"Smile! Say cheese!"

People take photographs every day to record special moments and events. But when it comes to the cameras they use, that is just part of the picture.

You may have had your picture taken today and didn't even know it. Special cameras take pictures of people at the bank, the store, and on the street corner. A camera on a **satellite** up in space might be snapping photographs of your neighborhood right now. If you get hurt or sick, your doctor might use a tiny camera to look inside your body to see what's wrong.

We'll be looking at several different types of cameras—some that take still photos and some that record hours and hours of video. Before we're done we'll see lots of ways people use cameras to get a closer look at the world.

mini camera

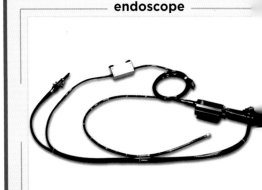

endoscope

35mm camera

digital camera

satellite with camera

microscope with camera

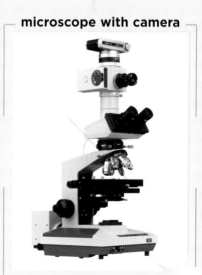

3

Chapter 1: Crime-stopping Cameras

Video cameras are powerful crime fighters. Many stores and businesses use video cameras to stop shoplifting. You may have noticed a small camera pointed toward you in a store. These cameras are recording everything they see. This is called video footage. Security guards watch the video footage to make sure everything is OK.

These video cameras help stop crimes from happening. People who know that they'll be caught on film will be less likely to do something wrong. If someone actually does rob a store, police officers watch the video footage to see who the criminal is. When a camera is used this way, it's called a **surveillance** camera.

This photo was taken by a surveillance camera in an art museum.

High-tech Video

When video cameras were first invented, they were big and heavy, and the pictures they took were not very good. But the newer cameras of today are much better. The images are clear and sharp. New technology makes it possible for these images to be sent through cables and telephone lines to places many miles away.

Some video cameras can turn in every direction. Some are equipped with heat-sensing devices, motion detectors, bulletproof cases, and even small wipers in case it rains or snows. These video cameras are also much smaller than the older ones. Most of the video cameras you can buy at the store fit in the palm of your hand.

Have you had your picture taken today? Think of all the places you've been—could there have been a camera pointed at you?

Safe at School

Some schools have begun using surveillance cameras for the safety and security of their students, teachers, and property. For example, schools often have expensive equipment, such as computers, that burglars might want to steal. Using video cameras, security guards can keep an eye on things even when the school is closed.

Police officers use surveillance cameras to take pictures of possible criminals and collect evidence of a crime. They often use tiny cameras, some as small as a dime. These cameras are easily hidden in things like a baseball cap, a watch, or even in a pair of sunglasses!

A student security officer videotapes high school students in a courtyard during lunch hour.

Hidden Cameras, Public Places

To cut down on crime, some communities have set up cameras in public places. Sometimes these cameras are hidden, and sometimes they are in plain sight. On street corners, in parks, in parking garages, and in subway stations, these cameras record people as they come and go.

The video footage from these cameras is sent to TV monitors where police officers watch to see what happens. An officer who sees a crime in action quickly calls the officers who are close by, describing the suspects to them. Those officers can then make a speedy arrest.

Some people think it's a bad idea for cameras to record what we do without our knowledge. Can you think of a reason why they might feel that way? What do you think?

This security officer watches the video footage from several surveillance cameras at once. If he sees a crime take place, he reports it to other officers who make the arrest.

Chapter 2: Satellite Cameras

Imagine a camera up in space that can take pictures of the Earth's surface that are clear enough to show the difference between an oak tree and a pine tree. This kind of camera is called an **imaging satellite**. Imaging satellites are blasted into space aboard the space shuttle. While orbiting the planet, the satellite snaps pictures of places and things with its **digital camera**. These pictures are sent back to Earth and received at ground stations.

Imaging satellites are often used for watching the weather here on Earth. These satellites photograph clouds and storms and send the information to weather stations. Based on the movement of the storms, scientists can make guesses about what the weather will do next. This is very important when storms like hurricanes and tornadoes are in the area.

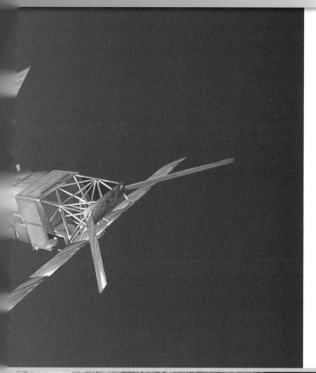

I Spy, You Spy

Spy satellites were first used in the 1960s. By taking pictures from space and beaming them back to Earth, countries at war could gather information about each other's tanks, airplanes, weapons, and military bases. Today, new kinds of imaging satellites deliver much sharper pictures. Even in peacetime, governments use these pictures to watch one another.

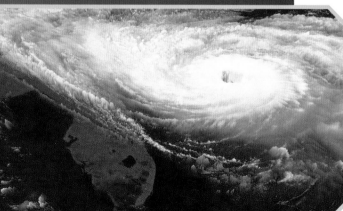

This is a satellite image of a hurricane off the coast of Florida

The Big Picture

There are many ways to use imaging satellites. Scientists use satellite pictures as a way of looking at our planet. By studying pictures of forests that have been taken over long periods of time, researchers can see which kinds of trees are growing and how healthy the forest is. Earthquakes and other natural disasters can also be studied using satellites.

Satellite pictures give a sky-high view of cities, oceans, and crops. They provide information about the places where people and animals live, helping those researchers who study population growth. In the future, satellite images might be used by farmers to check on their crops, or by fishing boat captains to spot schools of fish.

Someday soon, you might be able to see up-close pictures of your own home or your favorite vacation place that were photographed from space.

Scientists use satellite photographs to study how areas of the planet change over time.

Satellite cameras can zoom in very close to take pictures of the planet's surface. This photo is of part of the Andes Mountains in South America.

Did you know that anything that orbits Earth is called a *satellite*—even the moon? But most people use the word *satellite* to describe a spacecraft that is launched into space by humans.

13

Chapter 3: Infrared Photography

Some cameras can do more than just take a picture of what something looks like. They can also photograph light that can't be seen by the human eye. This is called **infrared imaging**.

An infrared camera can take pictures in total darkness. It can see heat energy coming from an object, then it changes that energy into a picture. The warmest parts of the object show up as dark red areas. The cooler parts are green and blue.

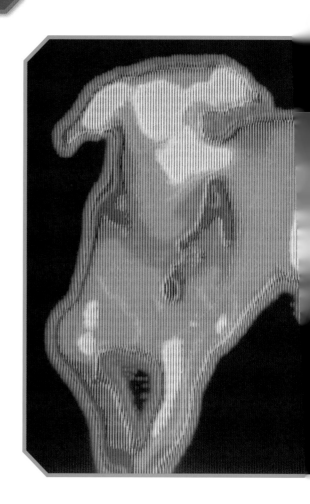

If you used an infrared camera to take a picture of a black dog at midnight, the warmest parts would appear red and yellow, while the coolest parts would look green and blue.

This image of the rings of Saturn was taken by an infrared camera onboard the spacecraft Cassini. The different colors show the different temperatures of the rings.

Warm and Cool Images

Infrared photography can be used in some interesting ways. The U.S. Forest Service uses infrared images to locate and track forest fires. Wildlife scientists use them to count animals. The animals appear as bright spots of color in the dark woods. When people are lost in the wilderness, search-and-rescue crews use infrared cameras to help find them in the dark.

In Idaho, the U.S. Forest Service keeps track of the health of trees with infrared photography. In this infrared photograph, the red trees are healthy and the gray trees are dead.

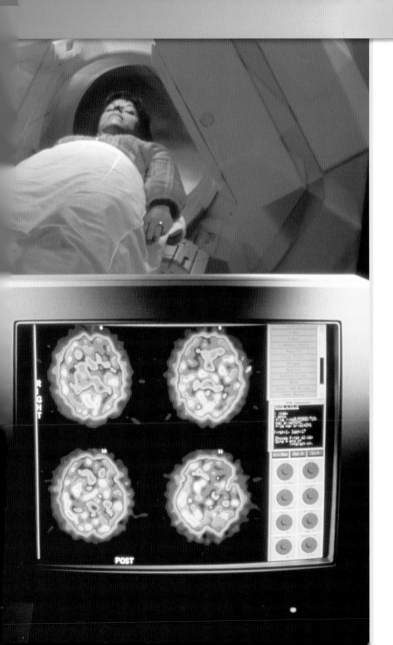

Veterinarians and ranchers also use infrared cameras to check on the health of their animals. Those that are sick or not eating well give off a cooler image color than healthy ones.

For people, doctors use this imaging to find medical problems like toothaches, migraine headaches, and nerve injuries. They can also find cancer cells and tumors. These sorts of diseases show up like red hot spots in infrared pictures.

Doctors use infrared imagining to look inside this woman's skull. The different areas of her brain show up as different colors of warm and cool.

Revealing What Can't Be Seen

Researchers use infrared cameras to study documents that are very old or have been damaged and can no longer be read. Used in this way, infrared imaging is a tool that can help solve ancient mysteries. The Dead Sea Scrolls were written thousands of years ago, and the writing was much too faded to be read. What did the Scrolls say? Infrared imaging was used to photograph where the ink had been, so they could be read once again.

Infrared photography can even help experts solve crimes. Infrared pictures can show signatures on written documents like wills or checks that were erased or written over. This technology can also show "fake" signatures on paintings. These powerful cameras can see what the human eye cannot.

Now you see it, now you don't! What does the infrared photo on the right show you that you wouldn't be able to see with your eyes alone?

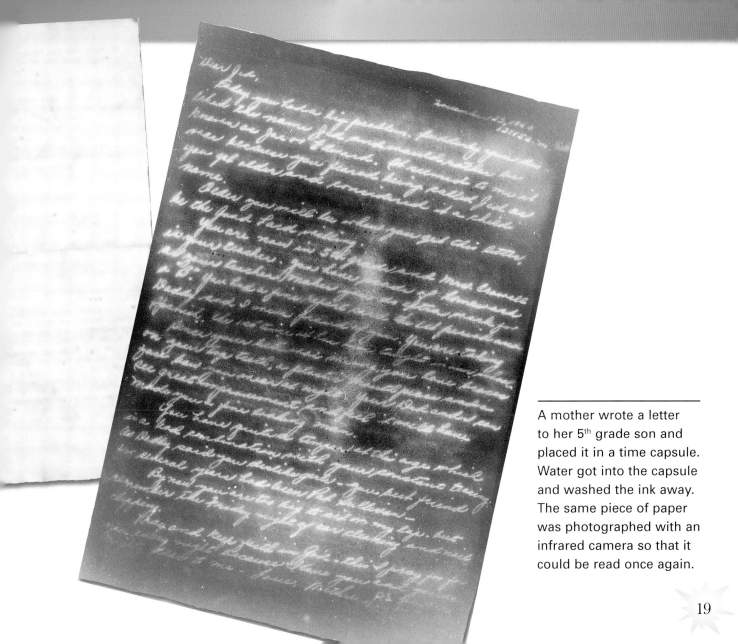

A mother wrote a letter to her 5th grade son and placed it in a time capsule. Water got into the capsule and washed the ink away. The same piece of paper was photographed with an infrared camera so that it could be read once again.

Chapter 4: Cameras Inside Your Body

Imagine being able to see inside your body—to watch your heart beat or to look at what's inside your stomach. That's what doctors can do with a special camera called an **endoscope**.

The endoscope is a long, thin tube with a tiny video camera and light on the end. The endoscope is as thin as a pencil lead and is no bigger than most of the food you swallow! The picture from the endoscope's camera is shown on a monitor for doctors to see.

Doctors use endoscopes to search for problems that may require treatment. Also, by using an endoscope during surgery, doctors can make smaller cuts in a patient's body than they did before. This helps the body heal much faster.

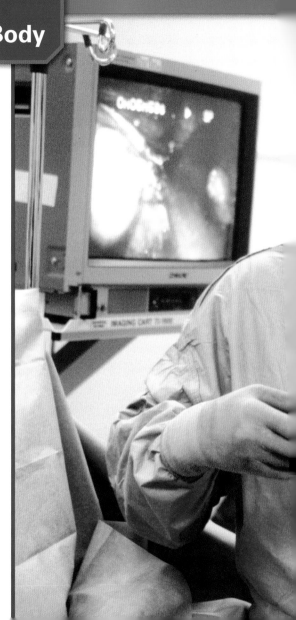

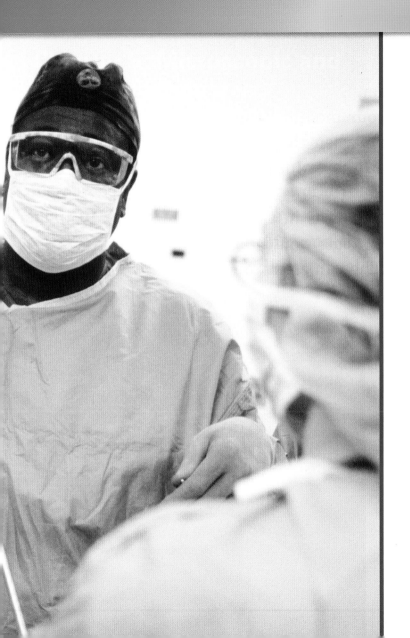

Time for Your Pill

Being able to see inside your stomach is as simple as swallowing a pill. Scientists have invented a dime-size capsule that contains a tiny camera. As the pill makes its way through the body, it sends images to a computer. The new camera pill allows doctors to see everything inside your stomach and intestines!

The endoscope and the camera pill are just two of the ways that new camera technology is helping doctors treat their patients.

Cameras in Space

Did you know that there's a telescope whirling around Earth that's the size of a bus? It's called the Hubble Space Telescope, and it's taking pictures of planets and stars. It sends these pictures to scientists on Earth. The scientists study the pictures to learn new things about the universe.

The Hubble Telescope travels at 5 miles per second, which means it goes all the way around the world every 97 minutes.

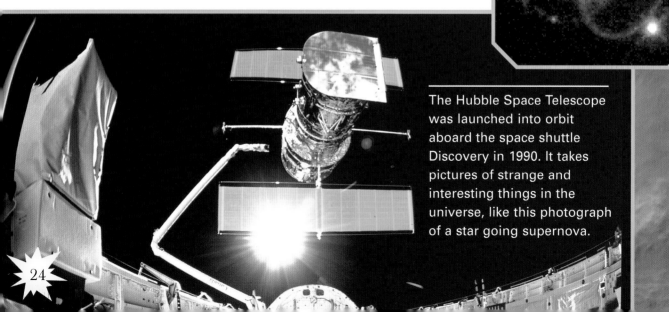

The Hubble Space Telescope was launched into orbit aboard the space shuttle Discovery in 1990. It takes pictures of strange and interesting things in the universe, like this photograph of a star going supernova.

Mars to Earth

NASA has sent several ships into space equipped with **telescopic cameras**. One of these, a spacecraft called the Mars Global Surveyor, has been orbiting Mars and taking pictures since 1996. These pictures have shown us some amazing new things about the "Red Planet."

For many years, scientists thought that Mars was a very dry place. Now, new pictures of the planet show that thousands of years ago, Mars may have had water on the ground in lakes and streams. This is just one way that the telescopic cameras out in space are helping us solve the mysteries of the universe.

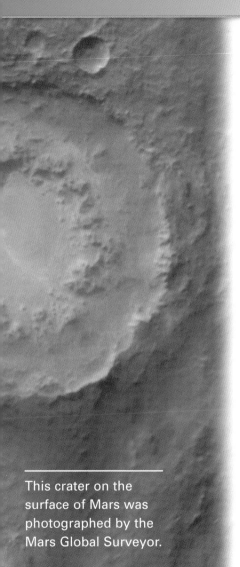

This crater on the surface of Mars was photographed by the Mars Global Surveyor.

Why do you think scientists want to know if there once was water on Mars?

If you've ever seen an IMAX® movie, you know how exciting it can be! These movies are made with extra-large cameras and extra-large film. IMAX cameras can weigh up to one-hundred pounds each. The film is ten times larger than the film that most people use in their cameras at home. The larger the film, the sharper and clearer the picture will be.

IMAX movies are shown on giant screens that are as tall as an eight story building! The sound is recorded on a special recorder with stereo sound. This means that the sound is coming at you from every direction, not just from the movie screen. When you watch one of these movies, it feels like you're right in the middle of the action.

This IMAX cameraman is filming climbers on Mt. Everest.

IMAX cameras have filmed amazing things and places. They have gone underwater to film the *Titanic* that sank into the Atlantic Ocean in 1912. They have gone to the top of Mt. Everest in southern Asia, the tallest mountain in the world. They have been flown into raging fires and erupting volcanoes to capture nature's fury. These cameras have even been on space shuttle missions into space.

A special IMAX camera was put onboard the International Space Station in orbit around Earth. The astronauts had to be trained to use the cameras and to handle the large reels of film.

27

Instant Replay

Were the player's feet in-bounds when he caught the football? Did the puck go into the net? If you've ever watched a sporting event on TV, you've probably seen an instant replay.

An instant replay lets us take a second look at something that just happened. Several cameras shoot the action from different angles to be sure that they get as much footage as they can. This footage is then sent to a TV studio, where only one of the pieces of footage is chosen and shown to the audience—all within seconds!

How an Instant Replay is Made

The action is filmed from several different places.

The footage is first sent to a satellite, then to the TV studio.

The instant replay footage is selected.

The instant replay is shown to the audience.

What's Next?

Cameras are all around us. Some are as big as a bus, while others are as small as a quarter. Some cameras can take pictures in the dark, and some take pictures of things that are too small to be seen with the human eye. Special cameras can even see colors and light that are not visible to human beings.

Scientists continue to invent new and exciting ways to see the universe and to solve its mysteries through the eye of a camera. Can you imagine what cameras will be able to do next?

Comparing Cameras

The Science of a Photograph

When you take a picture of something with a camera that uses film, light bounces off the object and into the camera's lens. When you press the button to take a picture, a shutter is opened. A shutter is like a window shade. While the shutter is up, light shines onto the film. The film undergoes a chemical change and an image of the object is burned onto the film. It all has to do with light and chemistry!

How a Digital Camera Works

Digital cameras are sometimes called *filmless cameras*. Instead of using film, a digital camera takes a picture, then it turns the image into computer code. A computer then changes the code into a digital picture and shows it on a computer screen.

Glossary

digital camera
a camera that takes pictures in computer code instead of on film

endoscope
a long, thin tube with a tiny video camera that doctors use to take pictures of the insides of their patients

imaging satellite
a space camera that takes pictures of Earth, other planets, and stars

infrared imaging
photographing light that can't be seen by human eyes

photomicrograph
a picture that is taken through a microscope

satellite
an object that orbits the Earth

surveillance
close watch kept over a person or object

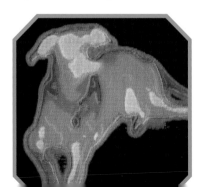

telescopic camera
a camera that can take pictures of things that are miles and miles away

31

Index